A
Slice of
Pineapple

A Slice of Pineapple

Copyright © 2008
by Mary Louise Uchida

All rights reserved.

Library of Congress Number: 2008941899
International Standard Book Number: 978-1-60126-157-1

Printed 2008 by

Masthof Press
219 Mill Road
Morgantown, PA 19543-9516

Table Of Contents

The Wrinkled Lady 1

Fried Mosquitoes 7

Jungle Rain 10

An Inconvenient Communication 21

Cockroaches Come With the Territory 25

Background 28

Five Thousand For Dinner 34

Bruce, The "Dumb" Horse 36

80 Amps 45

Lord, Do I Have To Have Whiskers? 49

Survival in the Jungle 52

The Three-Second Rule 61

Something Eggstra 65

The Cat and a Rock 68

There's a Carrot Out There 74

Horse Etiquette 77

Moving is a Many-Blendered Thing 79

Moved by an Ant 84

A Happy Farmer Smile 88

Surrounded by a Rainbow 93

Mary Louise and Mel at their farm in Hawaii. Photo credit: Mike Uchida

Acknowledgments

(This is where I get to say thank you to everyone who helped me!)

I am grateful to . . .

- **God**—for making me write…. for helping me to write . . . and for giving me the opportunity to publish a book. Without Him, this project would not have gotten off the ground.

- My husband, **Mel**—otherwise known as "Hubby". He has been an inspiration—sometimes as the basis for a story! He is a good *sport* . . . as well as a good *support* for this project. *Thank you, Hubby*!

- **Karen Gearhart**—friend and relative. Karen's laughter and warm encouragement gave me confidence to continue writing after a tentative beginning. Additionally, her helpful literary suggestions improved the final draft. Thank you, Karen!

- **Others—friends and relatives.** Thank you for your support and prayers. Thanks for listening to my stories, and for cheering me on! Hey…. it's done!!

Introduction

(Or.... "The Reluctant Writer")

I did not set out to write a book. Writing a book is what someone else does. If I had to explain why I wrote this book, however, it might go something like the following:

One day God said, "Mary Louise, I want you to write."

M.L. said, "Who . . . me? I can't write . . . never could write. I hate to write."

Some months later . . . God said, "M.L., I want you to write."

M.L. said, "You know I can't write. Writing has always been extremely difficult for me. It still is. I *hate* to write."

Many months later . . . God said, "Mary Louise, I want you to write."

M.L. said, "Okay already! But I need Your help."

With that, my writing adventure began. I was compelled to write, but at the same time reluctant to do it. The writing process did not come easily nor quickly. But as I became a willing participant, ideas started coming to my brain. I jotted them down. When a funny or inspirational situation showed up, something inside me whispered, "This would make a good story . . . " And so I wrote . . . .

When my friends kindly listened to some of my writings, they encouraged me to write more. Several dared to suggest that I should consider putting these "stories" into a book. "Why would anybody want to read a book by me?" was my response. Eventually though, the book idea prevailed. God provided a great publisher, and the rest . . . as they say, is history.

x

The Wrinkled Lady

The other morning I awoke with my head in a small black cloud. I had already been experiencing a mild depression due to some major life changes, but this particular morning was worse than usual. I tried to shake it off—or at least shake it to a place where I could ignore it—but I felt it settling in and I was powerless to stop it.

I could barely force myself to get ready for my physical therapy appointment in the nearest town 25 miles away. Somewhere during this struggle, a little thought pierced the black cloud. "You can ask God." It vanished in an instant, washed away by the black tide. A short time later though, the little thought reinserted itself. "You can ask God." This time it made an impression, but I hastily disregarded it, thinking, "Can't you see I'm depressed? Go away; I'm too busy being depressed."

But thankfully, the little thought persisted. I recognized its validity, but the only prayer I could muster up was, "Lord, please help me to feel better today." The prayer had an immediate and positive effect on my ability to function and the black cloud grayed a bit.

And now God was on the hook. I was curious to see how my prayer would be answered.

That day the physical therapy session ran longer than usual, leaving me very tired and quite hungry. I noted that I did not feel any better. The gray-black cloud lingered.

Next, I headed to the natural food store, a pleasant, but small establishment. Soon after entering, I became aware of a woman's voice—too loud, too friendly, and far too outspoken. When I went around the corner, I caught a glimpse of her and promptly noticed that she was also far too wrinkled! She had wrinkles everywhere—not just ordinary wrinkles, but countless deep furrows ran across her face and her arms—the kind of wrinkles that result from too much sun exposure or from too much smoking. She was not elderly, nor was her hair gray, and she exuded energy.

Secretly, I comforted myself with the fact that I have far fewer and much less-noticeable wrinkles. I steered away from her, my mood dictating a need for peace and quiet. But soon I discovered that I could not avoid the wrinkled lady. No matter which aisle I chose, it seemed she would be at the other end of that aisle. Or vice versa. (Of course, the fact that we were in a small store had nothing to do with it!)

Eventually, I finished my list and headed to the check-out lines. I could not believe my eyes. The wrinkled lady was checking out too and there was not one person behind her, but there was a whole line of customers in the next (and only other) lane. It appeared there was a quiet conspiracy operating to leave me with two equally unpleasant options—long, long line, or line up next to the Wrinkled Lady.

Because I was tired and wanted to get out the door and on the road, I stifled the temptation to stall, and bravely unloaded my groceries onto the belt next to her groceries. I carefully placed a divider between her stuff and mine, and pretended I didn't notice her. It was easy to do this at first, because the gregarious Wrinkled Lady and the young, bubbly cashier were chatting happily. In spite of my resolve to the contrary, I found myself drawn into their banter when they started raving about the succulent grapes on sale.

After I had made an emergency dash for my very own bunch of grapes, I withdrew to my previous air of detachment. Meanwhile, the Wrinkled Lady was preparing her payment, so I thought nothing of it when the cashier started to scan my own items.

Suddenly, the cashier, pointing to my groceries, said, "Are these yours?"

I said, "Yes."

Wrinkled Lady said, "No."

Consequently, the bouncy, distracted cashier had to undo her mistake of adding my groceries to W.L.'s tab! Again I was reluctantly drawn into the conversation. And now, this cashier (very young, and obviously with incredibly poor eyesight!) made her, no-doubt, biggest blunder of the day. She looked at W.L. Then she looked at me. "Are you two sisters?" she queried. I gave her a stunned "NO" and she continued, "Well, you could be. You look just alike."

I could not believe my ears!! Any feelings of friendliness that had budded in the previous five minutes instantly evaporated and were replaced by a stony coldness. I didn't know whether to laugh or cry. How could she say such a thing?? There was NO, I repeat, NO way we could even begin to look alike! I know I might be a bit sensitive about my age, since I recently joined the 60+ group, but really, the W.L. and I? Please!!

And furthermore . . . "God, if this is your idea of Something-To-Make-Mary-Louise-Feel-Better-Today, I gotta tell You, it's not working. . . ." But somewhere inside of me, I heard laughter, but only a little. Thankfully, the rest of the day's errands brought nothing unusual and I eventually arrived home.

The black cloud finally lifted that evening—quietly and without fan-fare. God did answer my prayer and what's more, He gave me a memory and a chuckle too!

Fried Mosquitoes

Among other visitors to our barn-house, we occasionally entertain a crop of mosquitoes. These are unwelcome any time and are particularly annoying at the critical moment of just falling asleep.

The other night a fresh batch of mosquitoes invaded the premises—undoubtedly due to a door inadvertently left open at twilight. As they settled in for a feast of our flesh, we accepted the challenge and mounted an attack of our own. Initially, we were slapping and clapping, but soon found we were no match for these elusive creatures. That's when we decided to go for the big guns.

My husband, who loves gadgets, tools, and tinkering, had previously invested in a racquet-like contraption designed to kill bugs mid-flight. This specialized racquet is strung with wires and powered by batteries. By the squeeze of the handle and a deft back-hand swing (or fore-hand), the unwitting mosquito is electrocuted in mid-air.

My hubby grabbed his "Weapon of Mosquito Destruction" and flew around, swinging his arms left and right, hitting some and missing others. I enjoyed watching the silly-looking, but very serious performance! During the course of the evening, he managed to eliminate most of the offenders.

Sleep time arrived, the lights were out, and the electricity had been turned off. As we lay in bed, we discovered the survivor mosquitoes. To my amusement, my husband grabbed the pre-positioned "WMD" and started combing the air blindly. Back and forth he swept the blackness above the bed. I giggled and moved out of range. Amazingly, in a short while, he had fried the remaining "buggahs" and we peacefully fell asleep.

. . . . .

No spiritual insights or analogies sprang to mind with this event. Just an entertaining evening!

Jungle Rain

It has been raining almost non-stop for a week now. Occasionally, the rain diminishes to a leisurely drizzle, but appears unable or unwilling to bring itself to a complete stop. I have emptied the rain gauge numerous times. As of now, the grand total for the past few days exceeds 30 inches!

I have never seen so much rain here at our farm. We have a seasonal stream on the property, but it is often dry or stagnant. Now, when there is a lull in the rain, I can hear roaring rapids and thundering waterfalls. Our pond, ordinarily empty, is proudly overflowing. And still it rains. Any day now I expect to see little creatures lining up two by two in search of the ark! I have a new-found appreciation for the literary works of the distinguished poet who penned these immortal words: "Rain, rain, go away; come again another day...."

"Have I ever seen this much rain before?" I wondered to myself. Upon reflection, I recalled an intimate experience with a jungle downpour in Mexico.

Many years ago, as a missionary-in-training, I traveled to the jungles of southern Mexico to participate in a jungle living program. The 12-week course was designed to teach us how to survive and cope with primitive living conditions. We learned many skills such as food preservation, medical treatments, personal survival if lost, and how to speak the local language. Physical endurance—hiking, running, swimming, canoeing, mountain-climbing, and body-surfing the river rapids rounded out our training.

One of our assignments was a four-day excursion to a small village bordered by a grass airstrip. Each day had been carefully planned. On the first day, all the trainees (except mothers and children) would hike 25 miles to the village. On day two, the mothers and children would be flown to the village. These flights would also bring the food needed for the rest of the excursion. Day three would be a day of interacting with the villagers—party time! Day four everyone would be flown back to our base camp.

Our hike started off well enough. The mules carried our sleeping gear and food for that day and for the next morning's breakfast. We enthusiastically headed out with our seasoned guide and his trainee, a recent newcomer. All of us wore practical hiking gear including sturdy boots. (We women were required to wear skirts and blouses so we would not offend the eyes of any local native Indians). We each carried a canteen of fresh water, a compass, and the ever-present machete. The skies were sunny and beautiful. We sang and "talked story" as we hiked . . . and hiked . . . and hiked. Lunch on the trail tasted extra-delicious.

At day's end, we arrived at the edge of the village and set up camp near an empty, thatched-roof, pavilion-like structure. After a yummy meal (wish I could remember what it was), the day was over and we each retired to our individual sleeping quarters—an army-styled hammock hung earlier between two competent trees. The surprisingly comfortable hammock was constructed in the shape of a long covered box with windows along the sides. It provided the user with his or her own private space—a hanging bedroom, as it were. Complete with built-in netting, it protected the user from the malaria-carrying mosquitoes—and other pests.

Because of the strenuous hike, I fell asleep instantly. During the middle of the night, I awoke when it began to rain. Snug and dry, I soon drifted back to sleep, but the rain continued the rest of the night. Thankfully, my hammock roof didn't leak. The next morning it was still raining. The leaden skies threatened an all-day downpour.

We cooked our oatmeal breakfast over an open fire. As the morning wore on, we began wondering aloud about the prospects of planes being able to fly in that weather. We thought about the folks who remained at the "home" camp who were waiting to fly to us. We thought about the food that those same folks were planning to transport to us.

The continuous rain answered our questions. The airplanes would **not** be coming. Since we had carried with us just enough food to last until the planes arrived, the cancelled flights also cancelled our meals!

Our group leader quickly grasped the nature of the problem facing us. He rose to the challenge. He and his leader-in-training headed into the village to buy something for us to eat. They returned later with a number of live chickens. Oh great, I thought. Now we have to butcher chickens! I was in no mood to proceed with that project.

The leaders issued one chicken per three persons. "The rest is up to you," we were told. The abundance of rain and lack of food eventually overcame our reluctance to do the dreaded chore. In a brief "committee meeting," our group of three determined who was going to do what. An hour later we were enjoying a delicious chicken dinner!

The rest of our time there blurs in my memory. (After all, it was more than 30 years ago!) There was not much to do. The only dry areas were the hammock and the center of the small, open-sided pavilion. Clear in my memory, though, is the fact that the rain poured on, unabated. After two full days and two full nights of unrelenting rain, my hammock, formerly my friend and dry haven, switched loyalties and sided with the rain. The once-trusty hammock sprang leaks here and there.

In time, the lack of food, the sloppy-wet campsite, my leaking hammock, and other inconveniences took their toll on my attitude. Grumbling became my companion. I hated the rain and our unfortunate circumstances. I didn't want to be there. I was miserable.

I suppose others were miserable too, but my own bad attitude is what I remember!

Because of the rain, we never did make the trek into the village for "fun and games". The food-bearing airplanes never arrived and the other promised joys of the weekend never materialized. A wretched failure. At least, that was my assessment. Looking back, I suppose the experience taught me something valuable, but at the time I just wanted to be dry and warm with a well-fed tummy.

During the third night, the rain finally stopped. The next morning dawned bright and clear. The more-than-welcome sun greeted the day—the day of our return to the base camp. The sky above the tall jungle trees boasted a gorgeous shade of blue, shining with hope and promise.

Everyone's spirits lifted as we broke camp and packed up to leave. The short flight back to camp would provide the relief we sorely needed. But our leaders realized the truth. The airstrips were too wet. There would be no flying that day either. The only way home for us was a 25-mile hike.

Having come to grips with our fate, we made the best of it and mentally prepared for the trek. Tired, hungry and damp, we began our journey "home".

As I recall, the first part of the trip proceeded uneventfully. We made good progress. As time went on, however, the trail began to degrade. It continued to degrade until eventually the trail became a vast sea of mud which extended ahead indefinitely. There was no way to go around it or beside it. It could not be avoided. We were forced to trudge right through it. This mud was not just ordinary mud . . . it was jungle mud . . . with a mind of its own. Every step I took, it sucked and pulled at my boots.

The miles and miles of mud hindered our progress noticeably. It didn't take long for the grumbles to set in once more as my knees and ankles protested in pain. Every step required a great deal of effort to pull my feet out of the 10-inch deep mud.

Somewhere along the way, our large group was divided into two smaller groups. Our group inherited the leader-in-training whom I already didn't like. He also had less jungle training than we did. All this added fodder to the grumbles inside of me as we trudged on down the mud-filled trail.

Sometime later, we sensed something was amiss. Not long thereafter, our inexperienced leader apparently sensed the same thing. He stopped us and announced, "We took the wrong trail. We need to turn around and go back." My sore knees and ankles swore in disbelief! The inner, quiet grumbles graduated to verbal complaints as we turned around and retraced our mud-sucking steps. When we finally reached the proper trail, I was dismayed to discover that the correct trail offered its very own version of as-far-as-the-eye-could-see mud. The painful, laborious detour added another hour or two to the day's already long and torturous hike.

Mercifully, by the end of the hike, the trail had dried out considerably. When our primitive training-camp buildings finally appeared ahead, we knew we had made it. I stumbled into the yard, my clothes, my body, and my spirit heavily caked by the tropical mud. The mothers and children ran to meet us. They were excited and relieved that we were all okay and back home again. "We prayed for you!" they shouted. But my muddied heart scarcely appreciated their joyful greetings.

After a cold bath in the river and finally, clean and dry clothing, we were treated to a scrumptious dinner prepared by the women who had stayed behind. Afterwards, to our complete amazement, they served us delicious strawberry ice cream—a feat that surely competes with the seven wonders of the world! (To this day I have no clue how they were able to make ice cream in that remote place with no refrigeration or ice).

Thankfully, I quickly recovered from the trauma of that particular hike. A few weeks afterwards, we did a 35-mile hike with an overnight stop on the trail. I am happy to report that it did not rain; we had enough food; and everyone enjoyed the experience!

. . . . .

Back here at the farm, I know the heavy rains will subside. It won't always be this wet. However, I suspect the jungle rain some 30 years ago will trump the current rainfall—if not in actual inches, at least in actual memory!

An Inconvenient Communication

Communication can be tricky at times—probably most of the time. My hubby and I recently re-re-re-discovered this truth.

My cell phone rang one morning. I usually answer my own phone, but because I was temporarily "inconvenienced" and my hubby was near the phone, I asked him to please answer it for me. I needed but a jiffy to complete my task, after which I would be free to take the call.

He obliged, but I was annoyed when I heard him cheerfully announce, "Sure, here she is," and immediately attempted to hand the phone to me. Since he was aware of what I was doing, he surely could have concluded that I needed just one more second—or so I thought.

"I'm wiping," I protested in disbelief and minus the precautionary whisper that better judgment would have dictated. Hubby burst into silent, hip-slapping laughter as he held out the phone and waited for me to finish. As I took the call, I fervently hoped the caller (fortunately a friend) didn't hear my verbal protest. (At that time I didn't want to inquire, although she later assured me that she hadn't heard a thing. . . .)

Afterwards, I felt mildly irritated and asked H. why he tried to get me to take the call when it was clear (in **my** mind) that I needed just a few seconds more—at the max. After all, he could have easily said, "Just a moment, please," or something similar. He responded that he didn't know. I gently explained that I felt disrespected by what I perceived as lack of common courtesy, whereupon he sweetly apologized. I graciously (I hope) accepted and we both comfortably recognized that we were good friends again.

As I returned to my kitchen chores and he returned to his farm chores, I was buoyed by our successful handling of this mini-conflict, especially because it involved communicating verbally. Not long afterwards though, Hubby reappeared in the kitchen wearing an amused grin. "I remember now why I handed the phone to you," he began. Understanding that he had probably revisited our earlier discussion while he was enjoying the outdoors, I waited expectantly. He continued, "I was trying to help you by bringing the phone to you."

Knowing in my heart that he was telling the absolute truth, I was mystified. Then and only then did I grasp the extent of the miscommunication. He thought, perceived, spoke, and acted. I thought, perceived, spoke, and acted. The only problem was that we were not on the same page. I wonder how many times we think we understand each other and go on our merry way with nary a clue!

Days later I am still shaking my head, amazed that any valid communication occurs anywhere by anyone at any time—convenient or otherwise!

Cockroaches Come With the Territory

I hate cockroaches. They are ugly, dirty, and prolific. I can't remember my first encounter with a roach, but I have encountered at least a kajillion since that time.

Once while I was in jungle training in Mexico, our assignment was to hike several hours through the jungle and visit a small village for a day and a night. We three single women marched off and had a wonderful time with our "family du jour". When it was bedtime, we were given the guest sleeping quarters, which turned out to be a shed with some beds made out of sticks.

The night was most memorable—not only because of the rats crunching on the field corn piled in one corner—but also because of the abundance of cockroaches. They were literally everywhere. I spent the first part of the night brushing and swatting them away from me. As the night wore on, my efforts became futile, and I eventually capitulated, giving them free reign. (It is astonishing what you can put up with when there are literally no other choices). Miraculously, I caught a few winks of sleep and by morning, both the cockroaches and the ensuing nightmare were gone.

So you see, I do not, I repeat, I do not like cockroaches!

The other night I happened to see one—a small one—in our almost-completed bedroom in our barn-house in Hawaii. A few months earlier, I had seen one (and killed it of course) in the barn side of our building. But this most recent one was the first I had seen in our living area. I sighed and killed it. Later that very same night I spied his brother in the bathroom. Same reaction and same action.

With a sigh of resignation, I concluded that life in the beautiful tropics includes cockroaches—they come with the territory. And suddenly I had a glimpse of our lives as Christians. We are, in a sense, living in the tropics—we have been saved and are "seated with Christ in Heavenly places". We have intimacy with our God and Savior—paradise in this life. But then, along comes a cockroach—a nasty situation in our lives, an overwhelming problem, something annoying, something hurtful or something ugly, perhaps.

I am so thankful that Jesus helps us with the swatting and the handling of those cockroaches in our lives. And later on, we get the real Paradise and guess what? No cockroaches!

Background

Nearly every morning a few of us "girls" walk a mile or so for our health, and it always turns into a pleasant social event as well. We discuss a wide variety of topics and encourage each other regarding our respective life circumstances. Shoe-leather therapy, I call it.

On a recent walk, two of the gals were talking about the background noise that affects hearing-aid users. The word "background" was repeated several times and suddenly I remembered the time that I learned the true definition of the word "background". Of course I "knew" everyone would want to hear my "fascinating" story and I waited for just the right segue into the ongoing conversation.

Years ago my daughter decided she wanted to be a movie actress. To that end she pursued various acting opportunities including, among other things, working as an "extra" on various movies being filmed in our city. When she started working as an "extra", she was required to have a chaperone because she was under age. Since I already was her chauffeur, I chose to be her chaperone as well. She was paid for the hours spent on location and it didn't take long for me to figure out that if I also signed up to work as an "extra", I would get paid for my time as chaperone! Besides, it looked like fun and I quickly joined the "extra" pool and promptly began my new life as a movie star!—at least that is how it felt. In reality, I joined the "wannabes".

I was so excited my first day on location for a major motion-picture. We arrived at 6:30 a.m. in period costume that we threw together and hoped that it looked appropriate for the western theme. After signing in, we joined the other excited wannabe's in the waiting area—each of us hoping to be chosen to act in that day's shoot.

As the morning wore on and nothing happened, we chatted with our fellow competitors.

Everybody bragged about their past performances, past opportunities, and real-life movie-star encounters. Looking back, I wonder how much of it was true, but at the time, hey, it sounded good to us! Noon finally arrived at which time we were treated to a scrumptious catered lunch. We enjoyed the wonderful food and noted that meals like these would certainly increase the production budget!

After lunch, the director breezed in and wisely selected about a dozen deserving actors and actresses to help with the afternoon filming on the set. Of course we were thrilled to be in that group.

We walked onto the set, confident that our acting careers had just taken a giant leap forward!

The set was a restaurant and we were seated in small groups at various tables.

We were told to pretend we were having a pleasant dinner conversation, but not to make a sound. We rose to the challenge and after the cameras and lights were perfectly positioned, the filming began. It was fun to do our part while the professional actors were speaking and doing their thing. All afternoon we played our role of eating dinner out. With each "take", we improved our acting skills. We added realistic touches to our parts and enjoyed ourselves thoroughly. There were about four of us at our table. As I recall, the camera-man panned our table more often than he did the other tables . . . sometimes lingering for awhile (no doubt enjoying our stellar performances)! By the time the director was satisfied with all the "takes", which included various angles of viewing and many retakes, we had convinced ourselves that our futures included the Oscars and perhaps a star in the Hollywood Walk of Fame!

When the long afternoon drew to a close and it was nearing 6:30 p.m., the director called us to attention. We waited expectantly for our next "assignment". He thanked us for the afternoon's work and then barked out the next instructions. "Background can go home," he announced.

"Background can go home? What does that mean?" I thought. And slowly the light dawned. "Oh, I guess he means us . . . we are the background!" At that moment our fantasies of stardom collapsed and reality resumed its rightful priority. I will never forget that deflated feeling!

We didn't act any more in that particular movie, but we were paid well for our one day's work. We began to anticipate the day that the movie would play in the theaters. We had spent quite a few hours doing the restaurant scene and knew we would get to see ourselves on the big screen. *What a thrill that will be,* we thought.

The day finally came and the whole family eagerly went to see the movie. The movie was bad—bad plot, bad language, and a lot of gun-shooting. I did not enjoy it at all! But I forced myself to watch it anyway, hoping to see myself and my daughter on screen. We waited and watched through the whole miserable movie only to discover in the end that the entire restaurant scene had been cut!

"How fitting," I smiled, as my thoughts returned to the present conversation.

For by now, the discussion had drifted to other things and my untold story had faded…into the background!

Five Thousand For Dinner

This morning I read in Luke the account of the feeding of the 5,000. It hit me in new ways and encouraged me enormously.

The disciples perceived a problem: hungry people, no food

They approached Jesus with the problem and their own solution: Send them away.

Jesus threw it back to them: You feed them.

Their response: Impossible (we have very little food),

Cumbersome (we head to town and buy take-out for 5,000).

Jesus kindly gave them manageable tasks: Seat the people in groups of 50. The disciples were faithful in the small jobs.

Jesus put together the big job.

Bruce, the "Dumb" Horse

Bruce is one of two horses that share the land here at Ahelani Ranch. Umi is the other horse and assumes the alpha role. Bruce does not seem to mind playing second-fiddle, even when Umi literally pushes him around. Bruce enjoys relatively good health despite his advanced age. With dietary supplements, his arthritis remains under control, allowing him to walk and trot normally—although, come to think of it, I rarely see him trotting. In general, Bruce is laid back, pleasant, and gentle. He perks up when offered his prescribed concentrated (and apparently delicious) food. Behind his mild-mannered demeanor,

Bruce hides his intelligence. A few months ago Bruce enlightened us.

A barbed-wire fence surrounds our property. At the entrance is a temporary gate which originally consisted of two ropes and a metal post. How smart we are, we thought smugly. This is such a simple rope gate. The two horses can see the flimsy barrier, but they are too dumb to realize they could easily escape. Two strands of rope would be no big deal for these big animals. It's psychological, my husband assured me and I readily concurred.

When Hubby and I go to Oahu for a few weeks, Umi's owner comes to feed both horses. To make it easier for her, my husband rigged up two plastic garbage cans which contain a supply of food, supplements, and/or medicine. He secured these covered cans just outside the fence, but near the entrance to the driveway.

All proceeded as planned for a number of months. We fed the horses while we were on the premises. Umi's owner fed them while we were not.

One morning Hubby returned from horse-feeding and announced that there had been a break-in. Someone had accessed the garbage cans and removed a portion of the contents. Why they had not taken all of the food—or the whole can, for that matter—was a mystery.

At first we thought perhaps it was a kid playing a prank, but that didn't seem likely in our neighborhood. Next, we thought it might be a wild or stray animal, but that also seemed unlikely, because the tight covers had been removed. An animal could not cause that scenario at the garbage cans, we reasoned.

There seemed nothing to do about it at that point, except to secure the covers with rope. We also decided to keep our eyes open, and hope that it was a one-time occurrence. That decision made, we went about our normal farm living. That is, until a few days later, when Hubby discovered that the horse feed containers had once again been raided. This time even more food had been stolen. The thief had managed to remove the tightly-tied covers!

Shortly after the second theft, I was driving down our steep, one-lane road. I pulled over to allow an oncoming pickup to pass by. The driver (a neighbor) stopped, rolled down his window, and inquired about our horses. It seemed that another neighbor had recently observed a horse rummaging through the cans just outside our closed gate. The observant and helpful neighbor herded the horse back onto our property. Neighbor #1 wondered if we were aware of Neighbor #2's good deed. He also expressed concern about the errant horse—the dark one. He was talking about timid Bruce!

So now we knew who the thief was—Bruce, the Not-So-Dumb-Horse. How he had gotten out the gate and opened the cans still remained a puzzle. With the astonishing truth of Bruce's escape and thievery now in hand, Hubby took swift action to prevent another breakout. H. decided to chain both the top **and** the bottom of the moveable gatepost thus preventing Bruce from nosing his way beneath the ropes.

Hubby and I both felt better, knowing that Bruce could no longer escape, nor accidentally overeat. We went to bed that night, relieved that the mystery had been solved.

The very next morning, however, when Hubby walked out to the gate to feed the horses, he discovered that the newly-installed security feature was no match for Bruce who appeared to be getting smarter by the day! Bruce had escaped easily and was calmly munching horse treats from the pried-open-with-his-teeth can.

Clearly, a new approach was needed and we made a quick trip to the hardware store to get new and better temporary fencing. We were not yet ready to install the permanent farm-gate, so we looked for something cheap, but effective, for the interim. We settled on some construction-grade, heavy-duty plastic webbing.

Back at home, Hubby built a new and powerful-looking gate. Because it was lightweight, it was easy for us to move as needed for entry and exit at our driveway. Additionally, we rejoiced that it was wide and tall enough to keep Bruce in his place!

This new arrangement lasted only a few days before Bruce, the More-Clever-Than-Ever horse somehow managed to squeeze himself under the not-so-heavy-duty-after-all fencing. We found him once more at the feeding can! We could not believe it! We are dealing with a "professional", we decided, and scrambled to find yet another solution.

We had long-ago discarded our smugness and had gained a new-found respect for Bruce.

My hubby is clever too. Since our situation demanded an immediate solution, he hit on a wonderful idea. Using a roll of chain-link fencing, he unrolled two substantial lengths and laid them on the ground in front of our temporary gate. He explained that the horses would not venture to walk over this uncertain surface. It would keep the horses away from the gate, but still not hinder driving out the driveway.

This arrangement worked very well and we breathed easier. To our knowledge, Bruce did not venture onto the chain-link covered driveway even once. But the story doesn't end here.

One day soon thereafter, some friends from Colorado came to visit us. They drove up to our place in their rental car. I opened the gate for them to pass through. As I watched our friends drive in, I noticed that the chain-link fencing on the ground had begun to curl around the tires of the small rental car. I yelled and motioned for them to stop. The fencing was caught on something on the bottom of their car. They decided to reverse course to release it, but instead of releasing, the fencing became hopelessly entangled around the axle. They could move neither forward nor backward! The men all worked together and finally freed the car an hour and a half later.

Because of the chain-link episode that night, we knew the temporary gate needed yet another fix. The next day my determined hubby dragged away the now-hazardous chain-link sections. He took down the heavy-duty temporary plastic gate. He replaced it all with two strands of electrical wire which he hooked up to a solar-powered electric fence charger.

It does take a bit more effort to enter and exit the driveway now, since we have to turn off the charger, remove the ropes, drive through, re-hang the ropes and turn the charger back on. More importantly, however, Bruce does not escape! The horse food is secure.

We no longer worry about what the escape artist will try next.

. . . . .

Looking back, I realize we could have saved a lot of time, money, and stress, if we had chosen the electric fence option at the beginning. On the other hand, we would not have gained the deep appreciation that we now have of Bruce, the Highly-Intelligent-Horse!

80 *Amps!*

My life here at Ahelani Ranch sometimes borders on the surreal. We live off the electrical grid in an isolated area. Our water is free—rainwater straight from heaven (via gutters and a catchment tank). The sun provides our electricity. We have propane gas for the clothes dryer, the hot water, and the kitchen range.

One day I set out to do the laundry. I needed to do two loads. I wondered if we had enough electricity to do both loads. I thus inquired of the head rancher (my Hubby). "Yes", he replied. "The only problem might be the water. If the water pump kicks on while the washing machine is running, that would not be good," he warned. "It pulls 80 amps!!" Somehow that sounded ominous.

Pulling 80 amps means nothing to me. My brain fogs when amps, volts, and water pumps are discussed, but I knew I could trust his judgment.

The solution and obvious way to avoid a calamity of pulling 80 amps, overheating pumps and who knows what else, would be to fill the washing machine by using pre-pump water. Fine, but that means hand-carrying water from our giant water tank outside. We have two five-gallon water jugs. With only two or three trips to the tank, Hubby can carry enough water for both the wash and rinse cycles for one load of laundry.

My hubby doesn't seem to mind carrying all that water, and he quickly headed out the door—even though he was extra-busy on another project to make our life here easier. Instead of walking to the tank this time however, he creatively made the chore easier for himself by filling a water barrel lashed to the bucket of his handy-dandy tractor. He parked the tractor close to the door. Using the spigot he had earlier installed on the barrel, he soon filled the five-gallon containers and lugged them to the washing machine inside.

After the washing cycle started, my hubby once more filled the two containers and deposited them close to the washer so I myself could fill the tub when the rinse cycle showed up.

When it came time to fill the machine for the second load of laundry, I really didn't want to take Hubby away from his project. I decided to fill the machine myself. I could only carry half-filled containers and only one at a time. It took many trips to the barrel to finish the job. In the middle of filling the machine for the second rinse cycle, my mind wanted to take a bad-attitude detour. I remember thinking how much work it was and how much time it was taking.

Then a noble thought entered my brain. "At least I can." That little thought changed my thinking in an instant. I suddenly felt fortunate that my legs and arms work. I was grateful that I even **have** a washing machine. (After all, how many people in this world have to do their laundry in the river?) With my new attitude of gratitude, I finished the laundry with joy, a song in my heart—and minus an 80-amp disaster!

Lord, Do I Have to Have Whiskers?

Turning 50 was ok, but sobering. The thought of having lived half a century sounded serious. "You're-getting-old" thoughts began whispering darkly in my ear. I ignored them—for another decade!

Turning 60, however, forced me to consider the possibility that I might get old someday—not now, of course, but someday. . . . The words "Medicare" and "Social Security" forced their way into my consciousness. The term "senior citizen" mysteriously attached itself to my name—something that in my heart of hearts I never believed could happen!

Aches, pains and memory lapses began messing with my life. Even the mirror played tricks on me. I used to look in the mirror and see a nice woman—perhaps tired, perhaps not. Now when I look in the mirror, an obviously older woman peers back at me. "Who is that old woman?" I wonder. I don't wait for the answer.

One day I was feeling particularly sensitive about my senior citizen face. I needed to gather some photos for the TMJ specialist. (He needed a reference for my ongoing treatment). I found some appropriate, close-up pictures taken before the treatment began. I couldn't help noticing more than the shape of my jaw. One close-up picture revealed a row of strange, coarse, white hairs just below my lower lip. I was horrified! I had never seen them in the mirror . . . but then my eyes aren't as good as they once were!! With dismay, I dubbed them "whiskers," fervently hoping they were invisible to the rest of the world.

Later, that very same day, I chanced to read an article on how I as a "senior" should love my looks. In the article I was told to think about my inner beauty, to say positive things about myself, to set fresh goals, and to enjoy each day to the fullest. My guess is that these "helpful suggestions" were designed for the sole purpose of distracting me from thinking about my appearance!

That evening I quietly lamented my aging face. I peered into the mirror once again, which in turn prompted a conversation with God. "Lord, do I have to have whiskers? It seems a little bizarre that You would let whiskers grow on a mature woman. Wrinkles, I can understand, perhaps; they seem more natural. Grey hair, maybe. But whiskers? Lord, do I have to have whiskers?"

I didn't hear God's side of the conversation. I suppose that one day He will explain the joke to me. In the meantime, I will ignore (or remove) the whiskers. It's no big deal, really. I have more enjoyable things to do than to stress about a few silly female whiskers!!

Survival in the Jungle

Because of the remoteness of our barn-house at Ahelani Ranch, the work occasionally requires more of me than I think possible. I miss the conveniences of city life. (There, I admit it!) One day recently, a satisfying sense of accomplishment flooded over me at the conclusion of a heavy chore. That, in turn, precipitated a vivid memory of the time I "survived" in a remote jungle.

I have referenced in another story the jungle training I attended in Mexico. This jungle training involved, among other things, lessons on basic survival. Because of the possibility of getting lost in the jungles of our futures, our leaders wanted to make sure we would know exactly what to do in such circumstances. We needed skills that would keep us alive for a few days. Additionally, we needed skills to enhance our chances of being found by rescuers. Our instructors doggedly and patiently taught us these survival skills. The "final exam" for this portion of our training took place in the dense jungle that surrounded our camp.

I knew the final exam was pending, but what I did not know was the when. A real-life survival situation often occurs without warning. Consequently, to simulate the unexpected, we trainees were **not** told when we would have to go on the "Survival Hike". I knew a number of people who had attended this same jungle training in previous years. Without exception, all former trainees had survived the dreaded "Survival Hike". Even so, I still wasn't sure how I would fare when the leaders dumped me into the depths of the jungle . . . alone.

Finally the fateful morning arrived. We had just finished classes in a primitive lean-to structure, otherwise known as "the classroom". The instructor then calmly announced, "Girls' Survival Hike." With his announcement we were not permitted to go back to our stick-and-plastic dwellings to get any supplies or food. But because of our training, we each were carrying a water-filled canteen, a first-aid kit, and a trusty machete. All of these items we kept attached to strong belts which we faithfully wore.

No compasses were permitted when we set out. Our leader used a compass, however. I guess that was a good idea because he needed to be able to find us again! One by one each gal was assigned to a designated area with the words "right here is your spot." My anxiety built as we walked. Before long it was **my** turn. "Right here is **your** spot," I heard. I watched, as the leader, with the remaining women in tow, disappeared into the dense undergrowth. And then, . . . I was alone.

I was not frightened because darkness was many hours away and because I had many tasks to complete before nightfall. With vigor, I tackled the job of making a shelter out of branches, sticks, and vines. I chopped and gathered a supply of firewood for the night and stored it under my newly-constructed bed. By this time, I was fairly hungry and turned my attention to foraging. I discovered a root-plant nearby, (the only thing remotely usable, in my opinion). With the protocol I had been taught, I ascertained that this particular unknown plant was probably edible. I quickly built a fire. Using some of my precious canteen water I proceeded to boil the peeled root in my stainless steel canteen cup. Whatever it was tasted bland, but it satisfied the hunger pangs.

By nightfall I had accomplished all my chores. As I prepared for sleep, I wondered how the night would go. The friendly fire burned dutifully—to help keep away the wild animals. I enjoyed its warmth and the reassuring safety it represented. I made a mental note to keep feeding the fire so it would not go out during the night. I slept fitfully—a bed made out of sticks is not very comfortable. My mind stayed alert too, thinking about the fire. About half-way through the night, I could no longer sleep, although I was quite tired. I looked at my watch. I checked the firewood. Slowly, I came to the unhappy realization that at the present rate of consumption, I did not have enough firewood to last the rest of the night. After some quick mental calculations, I formulated a plan. I would use one log per each 15-minute block of time. By so doing, the logs would last until daylight.

It was then that I pulled out my New Testament and began to read. (How grateful I was that I had tucked a tiny New Testament and extra flashlight batteries into my first aid kit)! During that firewood vigil, I read quite a few chapters as the minutes slowly ticked away. Once, during that wakeful period, I heard an animal crunching through the underbrush, but thankfully, I saw nothing. Again I was grateful for the fire.

Finally morning dawned, and with the morning light came an exquisite sense of accomplishment. I had done it—maybe not perfectly—but I had survived an entire night alone in the jungle! The recognition of that accomplishment ignited in me a degree of confidence not known previously.

My newly-found self-confidence was put to the test later that morning when the instructor appeared. I was hoping he would tell me to dismantle my shelter and join him and the other "survivors" for the rest of the final exam—a task of practical problem-solving which would involve a simulated search and rescue operation. He didn't. He merely asked me how I was doing. Had I foraged for food? . . . (exam question, no doubt)! What had I done about finding an additional water source? . . . another exam question). I then showed him the small cut on my hand (self-inflicted while I was chopping firewood the day before). He administered some powdered antibiotic and complimented my efforts of self-treatment. Then he was gone.

Apparently, the rumor that sometimes the "Survival Hike" lasted two nights instead of only one night was true! I was disappointed, but had no time to wallow. I scurried to find more water, more food, and more firewood—plenty this time, I promised myself. All of these chores occupied my full attention the rest of the day.

Sometime during that day, a hamburger-sized beetle flew into my shelter. Hmmm, I thought, I could easily catch that thing and roast it. For by now I was quite hungry, having eaten almost nothing in the past 24 hours. I checked my hunger level. Nope, I decided, I'm not that hungry . . . at least not yet. The lucky beetle flew away before I could change my mind.

The remainder of that day passed uneventfully. I went to bed, slept little, and found myself reading my New Testament once again. Reading by flashlight near the fire was comforting. That long night passed and the new morning arrived, the morning of the third day. I had survived two whole nights alone in the jungle!

When the leader arrived that morning, he instructed me to tear down my beloved shelter. Hooray, I knew the hardest part of the "Survival Hike" was completed! I lost no time following his orders. When he returned sometime later, accompanied by the happily-chatting "sister-survivors", my area had resumed its wild and natural appearance.

We completed the rest of the final exam—the anticipated search and rescue problem. At the end we all returned to our huts at the base camp. We literally jumped into the nearby lake to bathe (much needed after all that hiking)! Later, we inhaled the mashed potato and steak dinners prepared for us by the guys! As I lay in bed later that night, I basked in the knowledge that I had done it. I had survived the "Survival Hike"!

· · · · ·

I will never forget the Survival Hike. More than 30 years later, I still retain positive effects of that confidence-boosting achievement—and some of the survival skills as well.

The Three-Second Rule

The other morning I dropped my dental bite guard on the floor. I was able to casually pick it up, wash it, and put it away without boiling it—thanks to the "Three-Second Rule". The "Three-Second Rule" is a maxim which states the following: "Something dropped on the floor does not get dirty provided it is picked up within three seconds after it makes contact with the floor."

Before I came to Hawaii, I had never heard of the "Three-Second Rule". I only discovered this valuable gem when a relative dropped a piece of food on our construction-zone floor. I was astounded when he promptly grabbed it and popped it into his mouth. When he saw my amazement, he enlightened me. He explained that the item had been on the floor for less than three seconds. "Everyone knows that things do not get dirty in that amount of floor time," he said. "It's the 'Three-second Rule.'"

With difficulty, my brain absorbed this piece of news. How could anyone believe such a thing, I wondered. I recalled my jungle training where we had been taught that dangerous germs abound on every surface. If something clean touches something unclean (such as the floor), then that formerly-clean something becomes unclean instantly. It must be thoroughly cleansed, if not sterilized, before using it—especially so, if that something is to be ingested!

The jungle training regarding germs and cleanliness has stuck with me over the 30-some years since it was drilled into my brain. Without being overly compulsive, I have been careful to observe the rules of cleanliness throughout the child-rearing days of my life.

However, when we began construction of our barn-house here in Hawaii, my carefulness evolved into an obsession. We shared the premises with mice and spiders and many other "unclean" critters. Construction-produced dirt and dust permeated every area. There was no way to keep things clean.

When I discovered evidence of mice in our make-shift cooking area, I had to bleach everything. I kept all utensils and dishes in air-tight containers. If clothing fell on the floor, it promptly went into the laundry basket. I wouldn't dare **sit** on the floor, much less **eat** something that fell on the floor! I would nearly freak out when things touched the floor or any other "dirty" area.

Thankfully, as time passed, my life calmed down a bit. The construction eventually concluded, and our living quarters assumed a comfortable degree of normalcy. The uncomfortable obsession diminished. I gradually adopted the "Three-Second Rule". In reality, I should probably call it the "Two-Second Rule" or perhaps even the

"One-Second Rule". In any case, my life is much improved. Thank you, Three-Second Rule!

. . . . .

Addendum:

When I started telling others about the amusing, but helpful, "Three-Second Rule", I discovered that nearly everybody already knew about it. How this vital information escaped my education, I will never know. The important thing is that I am now informed and up to speed with the rest of the world! I wonder what other helpful info gems I might be missing….

Something Eggstra

My husband has recently begun eating eggs again—something recommended by a health-care practitioner—because he needs more protein. In the past he did eat eggs, but had stopped, thinking it was healthier to avoid them. Back then, I was accustomed to making ordinary scrambled eggs and omelets for him. Now, however, the new protocol is for sunny-side-up eggs with runny yolks. It didn't take me long to learn the new style of preparation, and in no time I had mastered it.

One morning as I prepared to cook breakfast, my husband mentioned his "new and easy way" to prepare his daily eggs. He explained that while he was cooking for himself on his recent visit to our barn-house, he had perfected a way to fix his eggs. Furthermore, he noted, with his way they did not stick to the pan. Being curious and always willing to entertain ideas to improve my cooking, (especially if it entails shortcuts and helpful, easy cleaning tips), I listened to him explain the procedure in detail. I decided to try it immediately.

Accordingly, I put a small amount of water in a pan, carefully checking to make sure it was the prescribed ¼ inch deep. I added a teaspoon of vinegar. Then I turned on the burner and heated the water until it was almost boiling, but not quite. Perfect so far. I was following the regimen precisely. Then at just the right moment I ever-so-gently slipped the raw eggs into the simmering water. I placed the cover on the pan, and turned off the burner. The timer ticked off 3 minutes. I then removed the cover and looked into the pan.

Two perfect eggs looked back at me, but when I tried to transfer them to the plate, I discovered that they were determined to stick to the bottom of the pan. I searched my memory for solutions of past similar sticky situations. Using the information I found there, I was eventually able to remove the perfectly-done eggs. The eggs sustained surprisingly little damage.

After breakfast, I washed the dishes and started scrubbing the frying pan. My hubby happened to be standing nearby. I matter-of-factly commented that the clean-up with his egg-preparation method seemed to be much more difficult than with my method. Whereupon he casually offered, "Oh, I used a non-stick pan . . . " When I burst into laughter, he hastily added, " . . . but that shouldn't make any difference!"

All the rest of that day, I chuckled every time I thought about what had happened. I have told several friends the story and without exception, each has laughed merrily. However, to this day, my hubby still does not see the humor!

The Cat and a Rock

My life involves a fair amount of air travel—usually and thankfully, short flights. I can enjoy flying if I really put my mind to it and, of course, if I am confident of the Lord's protection.

Lately there has been a great deal of stress and upheaval in my life so on this particular travel day, I was not as relaxed as I might have been otherwise.

About mid-flight and without warning, a high-pitched noise pierced the drone of the jet engines and jarred my already-edgy nerves. The noise sounded like the urgent whistling of a boiling tea kettle. All the passengers noticed, but didn't seem bothered by it. I waited for the noise to go away, but as it continued unabated, my anxiety started to build. I noticed the flight attendant on the phone and imagined that she and the pilot were conferring about the loud whistle. Since I did not see the pilot rushing from the cockpit, I assumed all was well. But now I had to fight visions of the plane falling out of the sky and other such manufactured calamities!

I looked over at my unconcerned husband and had a bright idea. He is a retired airline pilot. Who better to ask about the ongoing, and nerve-wracking screech? I leaned over and asked him what he thought was causing that noise. My husband sensed my anxiety, but since he has had to live with an anxiety-prone wife for many years, he has undoubtedly wearied of assuring me that everything will be ok. In response to my question this time, my patient hubby raised a wary eyebrow and said, "Now don't let worry get started in you."

Too late for that, I thought. The anxiety has not only taken root and flourished, but it has matured and is now busy producing a new and bountiful crop! Furthermore, his gentle words of reprimand were not what I wanted to hear at that moment. I was thinking more along the lines of "Think nothing of it, My Love. It is merely a faulty coffee percolator . . ."

I knew Hubby was right, of course, and I bravely fought the anxiety alone. I searched frantically through my mind's repertoire of Bible verses for comfort, but because of the heightened anxiety, I could only think of one or two familiar phrases. I did remember, however, that only recently, a friend had given me a helpful verse and it was something about a rock. Although I could not remember it word for word, the promise that God was my Rock of safety brought a degree of peace to my heart. And I clung to that Rock.

The flight and the noise continued. I stole a glance at Hubby. He was asleep! How like Jesus, I thought. Sleeping, knowing all was well while the disciples were experiencing severe anxiety—

albeit they at least had a good excuse—their boat was in real danger!

Meanwhile we were approaching our destination and the pilot began the uneventful descent. The screeching noise finally and mercifully diminished a few decibels, bringing relief to my ears and my heart. At that moment I heard a cat meow. It was as if the cat missed hearing the whistling-whatever. And then it meowed again, a sad meow this time. Apparently the couple seated in front of us was accompanying their special and highly-valued cat to its new location and the cat had begun to voice its opinion of the traveling arrangements. The cat continued meowing, sounding more and more pathetic. She was obviously upset, not enjoying her current circumstances, nor knowing the outcome of her situation. Her owners began to speak soothingly to Kitty, but she ignored their attempts to comfort her. She continued her lament. By now I was feeling sorry for Kitty. I was glad that soon we all would be safely on the ground. There the owners could release Kitty from her uncomfortable and frightening surroundings, thereby restoring her peace and serenity.

I thought about the owners who clearly felt compassion for Kitty and her situation. They knew that she was okay and her discomfort temporary. They spoke lovingly to Kitty, but she didn't get it. I was musing about all these happenings. In a way, I identified with Kitty. Then the truth hit me…. that yes, I have been a lot like Kitty. My ongoing circumstances, including the current flight anxieties, have precipitated a lot of discomfort for "moi". Inwardly, I have been meowing a great deal. And yet God, my Owner, the Rock of my protection, knows I am okay. My discomforts are temporary. At this realization, I was overcome with emotion and gratitude as I glimpsed God's overwhelming love for me.

Shortly thereafter, the plane landed and rolled to a stop, safe and sound for both Kitty and the anxiety-prone wife!

· · · · ·

(The source of the noise remained a mystery, but I came away from that flight with a heart-felt appreciation for a cat and The Rock).

There's a Carrot Out There

One morning as my hubby and I were waking up, we began chatting about the coming week's schedule and activities. As we were concluding our discussion, I realized that we soon needed to get out of bed to begin the day.

I commented that I often feel like there's a little "somebody" inside me cracking the whip, forcing me to get going.

Because I know my hubby is a wonderful self-starter, I wanted to know what happens inside him that motivates him to get out of bed. I decided to ask him. "Do you have someone cracking the whip inside you too?" I inquired.

"No, its more like there's a carrot out there," he replied.

Wow, I thought. What a concept. Here I am in bed not able to sleep anymore because of all the many chores and projects clamoring for my attention. My hubby, on the other hand, is eagerly waiting to hop out of bed to get started on his projects and chores. (Frankly, I would rather be sleeping in!).

I wanted to hear more, however. I was hoping I could learn something from him to apply to my own, more negative way of thinking. Perhaps I could banish (or at least convert) the whip-cracker.

Because my hubby is a man of few words, I carefully forged a question designed to elicit a brilliant, detail-filled explanation. I asked him, "Would you please say another sentence about that?"

Whereupon he promptly stated, "There's a carrot out there."

I burst into laughter. "No," I said. "I wanted **another** sentence about the carrot".

"Well," he replied, "that was another sentence!"

Now we were both laughing. He matter-of-factly pointed out to me that his earlier sentences needed no further explanation. Still laughing, I gave up. I yielded to the temptation to translate his sentence into my own words. He finally helped me along by telling me that the "carrot" was the joy of getting his tasks accomplished. Period. End of story.

I came away with the following reflection: How much better it would be to view my work as a dangling carrot rather than as a pile of tiresome rocks. I look forward to many carrots in the days to come.

Horse Etiquette

Here at our farm paradise, there are two horses—DH and Nosey[1]. They do not belong to us, but while we are here, we like to pretend they are ours since they graze on our property and hang around our doors and windows with friendly horsey curiosity. We have come to enjoy them. We brush the dirt off their coats, treat their sores, and make sure they have water. From time to time we give them horse-healthy treats. They, in turn, seem to enjoy us as well.

---

[1] Not to be confused with Bruce and Umi who came to our farm after DH and Nosey moved away.

One day I heard a stomp or two and realized that one of the horses was standing outside our closed door. It appeared that he was stomping as a way of letting us know it was time for his "treat of the day." I was amazed—first, that he sensed the time of day; second, that he was communicating his desires to us and third, that he was acting in such a demanding manner. Granted, he could not actually verbalize his desires, but how about a soft whinny or a strong swish of the tail against the thin metal wall? We would have responded to either.

The net result of his stomping was a natural reluctance on our part to give out the treat just then. And then I wondered: How often do I act like that towards God? Just how many times do I approach God with a demanding attitude—subtle, or perhaps not so subtle?

The horses know that we care for them and want to give them good things. Likewise, my Heavenly Caregiver loves to give me good things, but how about an attitude of gratefulness when I make a request?

Moving Is a Many-Blendered Thing

I love to count. From my early years to the present, I have been counting things. I like numbers, but do not consider myself a mathematician. Perhaps counting is a way to keep things from being boring or to pass time, or even to allay feelings of anxiety, but the real deal is that I like to know how many. Perhaps I should have gone into the field of statistics, but that sounded uninteresting and besides, back in the days when I might have chosen that field, it certainly was not a "girl" thing.

As a kid I counted the cars in passing trains, counted cows in the fields, counted red convertibles, steps in staircases, boxes of freshly-picked (by me!) strawberries, people in choirs, number of minutes I could swing the hula hoop, and of course, the number of pennies, nickels, and dimes in my piggy bank! I counted countless different things. I even counted the entire flight of steps—all 897 of them—down the Washington Monument. (Thank God for the elevator that carried me up!)

When I had children of my own, I counted out loud with them—sometimes counting by 2's, 3's, and 5's to keep it interesting. As a parent, I used the count-down warning trick. I occasionally counted aloud while the kids were falling asleep. In time, they too learned to count cars in trains, cows in fields, and coins in piggy banks.

So it wasn't a huge surprise to me when I found myself counting items as I was unpacking our boxes shortly after our move to Hawaii. (Some of those boxes had not been opened since they were packed almost a year and a half earlier when we packed them up in Colorado . . . prior to moving to Texas . . . prior to moving to Hawaii). I discovered a number of unopened cartons of Q-tips tucked here and there. Apparently, once upon a time, at a completely irresistible sale, I had stocked up on Q-tips.

I collected all the cartons of Q-tips. There were 7 boxes. For giggles, I mentally tabulated the number of individual Q-tips—500 in this box, 350 in that one and so on. The grand total (including those in the opened box in the bathroom) added up to 3000—give or take a few! I couldn't believe it! My curious mind raced on. How long, I wondered, would it take us to use up those nearly 3000 Q-tips? After some quick mental math, I calculated that with our current rate of use, we owned enough Q-tips to last us nearly five years!! This is hilarious, I thought. What was I thinking?? Perhaps someday there might be a run on Q-tips? Or, perish the thought, they might stop manufacturing them?

With a light heart, I continued the unpacking process. I started to put away my husband's socks. Wow, he has a lot of socks, I noticed. I decided to count them. I included the ones already in use at the barn-house. The grand total—74 pairs of socks!! That's wild, I concluded. Who needs 74 pairs of socks? Certainly not someone who lives in a 600 square foot apartment inside a barn! I chuckled inwardly and kept working.

Over the next few days as I continued unpacking and organizing our belongings, I noticed various other "collections". I counted the washcloths—93 altogether! (How I collected 93 washcloths is part of another story). The chopsticks collection was too numerous and tedious to count (although I gave it my best shot. I gave up when the count reached 66 matched pairs and an unknown number of singletons.)! Among other things, I discovered that we had a total of 6 hairdryers, 48 disposable razors, 4 citrus juicers and 7, count them, 7 blenders!! A few of the blenders were the hand-held, so-called "stick" blenders, but that didn't change the glaring fact that we owned 7 blenders!

I was astounded at what we had collected—and carried with us—over the years. I was also starting to feel a bit foolish. What had happened to us? Had we unwittingly joined the ranks of the pack rats? My mind shifted into the self-defense mode. I began to consider the facts. There really is a logical explanation, I mused. It's because of all that moving!

We have made two major moves in less than two years. Besides that, since moving to Hawaii, we travel back and forth from the Big Island to Oahu every few weeks or so. Prior to those two major moves, we made extended trips from Denver—and later, from Houston—to work on our barn-house in Hawaii. Rather than toting household and clothing items back and forth, we purchased many duplicates—at garage sales, of course.

Satisfied with this sensible explanation, I casually threw away another Q-tip. 2,973 left to go, I thought, . . . but who is counting?

Moved by an Ant

When I went to the bathroom sink to wash my hands one day, I noticed an ant running around in the sink. Since all kinds of little creatures are a part of tropical living, I thought nothing of it. I was about to wash it down the drain when something arrested my attention. For some reason this did not look like an ordinary run-of-the-mill ant. Upon closer examination, I noticed that this particular ant was carrying something, and being curious, I looked even closer. It turned out that this little guy was carrying a fellow ant—a fallen friend, perhaps. His precious cargo was an injured or dead ant. I could hardly believe it. The ant was trying to rescue his buddy or carry his buddy's body to some more honorable place for repose.

Whatever the reason, I was overcome with pity watching the scrambling efforts of this ant that I had nearly washed away without a second thought. Now there was no way I could wash him down the drain.

Since I still needed to wash my hands, I decided to "help" the ant by scooting it out of the sink. Using a piece of paper towel, I pushed at him. When that failed, I cajoled him by presenting him with a paper towel for easy transfer of location. He refused my generous offer and rejected all my other kindly efforts to help him. He then dropped his cargo and started scurrying away in a frantic bid for his own survival.

Finally, seeing that all my efforts to help had totally failed, I went elsewhere to wash my hands and left him to his own devices.

I returned some minutes later to check on the mini-drama. I discovered that not only had my friend recovered from his self-defensive flight, he had dutifully returned to his task. He had retrieved his fallen buddy and was cautiously working his way up and out of the sink.

I withdrew again and went on to other things. When I next checked on him, both he and his buddy were gone, and I breathed a sigh of relief and wonderment.

This whole little incident gave me a deeper appreciation for God's gracious compassion. Of course, God's efforts to help me are much more effective and successful!

On the other hand, how many times have I (like the ant) been struggling, carrying a heavy burden—emotional or otherwise—and have been unable to see a God-given solution to my needs (because it is too scary or too strange). Furthermore, God is so powerful and large that He could easily "wash me down the drain", but He doesn't. Instead, He is filled with greater compassion for me and my struggles than the compassion I experienced (or could ever experience) towards Mr. Ant.

A Happy Farmer Smile

My hubby has always wanted to be a farmer—at least it seems like always. In reality, it was within the last 10 years that the farming fantasy showed up. Years ago, when we got married, I didn't know he wanted to be a farmer. Of course, neither did he. I was marrying a missionary and so was he. Life often takes unforeseen twists and turns, however, and now many years later, we embraced the possibility of a farming future.

We are now retired and have moved to our little "piece of heaven" here in Hawaii.

My hubby's dreams of being a farmer are bit by bit becoming a reality. We have a calf (Alphie), two grazing horses (not ours) and a struggling orchard of exotic fruit trees. Oh, and of course we have our barn-house and a tractor. Although we spend only half of our time at our "ranch", my hubby thrives here. Smiles abound as he tends to the chores and to various projects relating to developing and improving our farm.

Hubby's sister owns a piece of property about forty-five miles away from here. That property is another "farm-in-progress" where the new tenants are joyfully turning it into a wonderful working farm- -complete with gardens, trees, and soon-to-be-added, chickens and sheep. We drive over there from time to time to render assistance. (Hubby actually does the "assisting." I provide the "support", i.e. the food).

One day recently, H. excitedly prepared for one such journey to that farm. The day promised sunshine, a welcome proposition after a long stretch of rainy days. He was looking forward to working outdoors. He and the tenant planned to build a fence and a fold for the anticipated arrival of the sheep. To that end, my hubby happily packed his tools and materials and headed out.

My own plan was to get some work done at our barn-house before heading to town and later, up to the farm to join H. We were going to spend the night there so he could have two full days of work on site. (I'm still not brave enough to spend a night alone at our barn-house. I have not yet "tamed" the generator, the propane systems, **nor** the water-pump! Besides, I needed to transport the evening's dinner and the next morning's breakfast.)

Before I headed out that afternoon, the rains returned. I hoped and prayed that it would not interfere with Hubby's work project. It rained the entire twenty-five miles to town and continued in earnest as I did my errands there. Then as the rain poured on, I drove towards the farm. I wondered how the work was progressing, if at all. I called to let him know that I was on the way and he replied that he would open the gates for me.

The rain subsided and came to an end while I was en route. Within thirty minutes I pulled into the driveway and parked near the front entrance of the house. It was obvious that it had rained earlier. Hubby met me with a Texas-sized smile. "Now, there's a happy farmer," I thought, taking note of his yellow raincoat. "He's so happy working that not even the rain can dent his enthusiasm!"

Later that night after the generator, (and consequently, the electricity and the lights) had been turned off, I playfully aimed my flashlight at my husband's face. He smiled. It reminded me of the earlier Texas-sized smile and I asked, "Are you happy here?"

"Yes," he replied,

"I can tell you're happy," I told him, "because when I got here, you had a giant smile on your face."

Then my sweet hubby swiftly corrected me. "I was smiling at you!"

Surrounded by a Rainbow

I have been fortunate—blessed—to see many, many rainbows throughout my life. As a child, I was thrilled when we spotted a rainbow—especially after some of the horrendous thunderstorms known to visit our area of Ohio. My mother would show me a rainbow and point out that the dreaded and fearful storm had passed. Peace and comfort came with the appearance of the rainbow. Occasionally, but rarely, a second bow would form over the main rainbow. When that happened, it was an extra-special event—one to remember and brag about to our friends.

Currently, I live in Hawaii where rainbows abound. I never grow tired of seeing them in all their radiance. When my mainland friends or relatives visit, they invariably notice and enjoy the profusion of handsome rainbows. I have observed numerous double rainbows here with the second rainbow nearly as brilliant as the main one. Because of the intense colors, I sometimes wonder if there ever could be a triple rainbow—probably a scientific impossibility, but fun to imagine!

On rare occasions here in Hawaii (perhaps elsewhere also), the rain and a full moon interact to produce a nighttime rainbow. These night rainbows are not the same as the more common pale circle of light that occasionally forms around the moon. A nighttime rainbow is just that—a rainbow at night, formed by the full moon shining through rain. The colors in these "moonbows" are much more subdued, but that does not detract from their beauty. I have seen these unusual rainbows only twice in my life and I was thrilled both times.

My appreciation of rainbows rose to new heights yesterday. I was scheduled to fly to the Big Island again for the trek back to our farm after an extended stay on Oahu. As mentioned in another story, I have been suffering from depression and anxiety (thankfully it has improved). Accordingly, I was not surprised to notice an increased level of anxiety as I anticipated the flight and waited to board the airplane. One would think that a person who has flown hundreds of thousands of miles would not have anxiety about flying, but nevertheless that is what I was experiencing.

Proactively, I reminded myself that God has not given me a spirit of fear and that I am commanded to banish all anxiety from my heart. I prayed for my safety and pushed away negative thoughts. When I boarded the plane, I chose a window seat so I could enjoy watching the islands pass beneath my feet. Uneasiness still lurked in my mind, and I worked hard to extinguish it. I felt sad that my struggle even existed. I decided to ask God for permission to enjoy the flight. "Yes, yes, a thousand times yes," came the instant reply. But I was not prepared for what He had in store for me.

We took off into partly cloudy skies. As I enjoyed the shrinking scenery below, I suddenly noticed a nearby rainbow just ahead of the wing. "How cool is that," I thought, awestruck. "God sent me a rainbow to reassure me that all would be well!" I gazed at the lovely rainbow which now seemed to be following us. From my vantage point, it appeared that the center of the rainbow was positioned just outside my window. I marveled again, daring to believe that God, in His mercy and kindness had arranged to have that rainbow at just that place and at just that time because He knew that it would remind me of His care and promises.

Transfixed, I now observed that the colorful rainbow arc had extended itself into a complete circle! My wonder and amazement grew as the rainbow show continued. A smaller, light-filled circle developed in the center of the large circular rainbow. Precisely in the middle of that shiny circle appeared a perfect shadow of our airplane. The spectacular scene seared itself into my brain. I was overcome with emotion and the tears flowed—because God cared enough for me to place me in the center of a beautiful rainbow. It was a gesture that melted my heart and filled me with gratitude and peace. I thanked Him for sending all the rainbows and circles and the shadow of the airplane. I thanked Him for allowing me to witness this spectacular rainbow-show-in-the-clouds on a day that I so very much needed to know all was well.

The tears and the precious rainbow extravaganza evaporated, but the vivid memory of being surrounded by a rainbow remained with me for the remainder of the flight and will no doubt stay with me for the rest of my life.

. . . . .

The Sequel:

A few weeks later I returned to Oahu. My anxiety was less, but still active. Again I opted for a window seat on the plane and when we took off into a partly cloudy sky, I found myself scanning the clouds for another rainbow sighting. I didn't know if there would be one, but I was hoping. I started to see bits and pieces of color here and there, but no rainbow arc.

I did see a large disc-shaped brightness, but it was fleeting and not well-defined. Then something caught my eye. Almost directly beneath our plane I saw a small, complete circular rainbow—no, **two** complete circular rainbows, one nestled just inside the other one! I could hardly believe it! It was a double rainbow circle! As if that weren't enough, that gorgeous double rainbow contained a brilliant light which encircled—you guessed it—a shadow of our airplane!

The sight lasted only a few moments and then dissipated, but that was entirely long enough for me to appreciate this double dose of God's kindness and sweetness to me personally.

I was touched anew as I contemplated being surrounded by a rainbow—twice.